God's Promises of Prophecy

REFLECTIONS

ON GOD'S FAITHFULNESS

IN THE PAST

AND HIS PROMISES

FOR THE FUTURE

Dr. Jack Van Impe

COUNTRYMAN

Contents

Forward

$\mathcal{M}$uch of the Bible is prophetic. The entire Bible, including all the prophecies, is God's message to us. Second Peter 1:21 says, "For the prophecy came not in old time by the will of man; but holy men of God spake as they were moved by the Holy Spirit." This literally means the prophetic promises of the Bible are "God-breathed." What a blessing to know that God wants to reveal the glorious future to His creation!

The next step in that wonderful plan is the fulfillment of Jesus' promise to His disciples to come again as recorded in John 14:3. Christ's return is described as the "blessed hope" in Titus 2:13: "Looking for that blessed hope, and the glorious appearing of the great God and our Savior Jesus Christ." The happiness of the greatest event in world history has to do with seeing Jesus. If this thought does not bring joy and peace to one's heart, something is drastically wrong.

Multitudes today are unaware that there are two stages or phases within the process of the Second Coming—the Rapture and the Revelation—and that these two events are separated by a seven-year period of time. From what I have studied over fifty years, I believe the Rapture is the next occurrence on God's calendar. This Rapture is the literal, visible, and bodily return of Christ in the heavens (see Acts 1:9–11).

When Jesus returns in the heavens, all believers— dead and living—will also be taken bodily to meet Him in the clouds (see 1 Thess. 4:16–18). One day soon, the people of God are going to disappear from the earth in a blaze of glory!

The entire occurrence is going to take place in half a blink: "Behold, I show you a mystery; we shall not all

sleep [be dead], but we shall all be changed, in a moment, in the twinkling of an eye, at the last trump: for the dead shall be raised incorruptible, and we shall be changed. For this corruptible [the dead] must put on incorruption, and this mortal [the living] must put on immortality"
(1 Cor. 15:51–53).

Again, Philippians 3:20–21 verifies that our bodies will be changed as we enter into God's presence in whirlwind style. These verses tell us that "our citizenship is in heaven, from whence also we look for the Savior . . . who shall change our vile bodies, that they may be fashioned like unto His glorious body."

During the coming seven-year Tribulation that follows the Rapture, all hell is going to break loose on planet earth. It will be a furious time because the hindering power of the Holy Spirit—believers—will be temporarily gone from the earth (1 Cor. 3:16; 6:19). But as terrible as it gets on earth, there is still hope. In the middle of the carnage and destruction Joel 2:32 and Acts 2:21 give us hope because "whosoever shall call upon the name of the Lord shall be saved."

There is always hope in Jesus—then, and now. Christians should not be fearful and despondent, "sitting out" the next few years while history unfolds because we "know the ending of the book." We should not carry an attitude of despair and foreboding into our churches, our work places, and our family lives. Instead, we have cause for rejoicing in the truth. Why? Because Christ is first coming to snatch us away in the twinkling of an eye and then to return with us again to earth as He promised seven years later. We must expect His return at any moment.

It may be today. It may be tomorrow. But one thing is certain. God's "promises of prophecy" are sure, and Christ is coming soon!

Jack Van Impe

THE NATURE OFPROPHECY

All Scripture is given by inspiration of God, and is profitable for doctrine, for reproof, for correction, for instruction in righteousness, that the man of God may be complete, thoroughly equipped for every good work.

2 TIMOTHY 3:16, 17

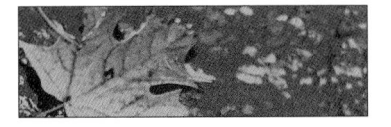

For prophecy never came by the will of man, but holy men of God spoke as they were moved by the Holy Spirit.

2 PETER 1:21

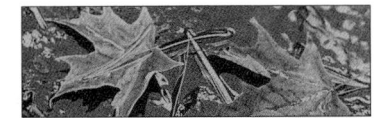

Men of Galilee, why do you stand gazing up into heaven? This same Jesus, who was taken up from you into heaven, will so come in like manner as you saw Him go into heaven.

ACTS 1:11

God's Promises of Prophecy

$\mathcal{P}$rophecy is history written in advance—and is presented by an individual, chosen by God, to speak forth God's message to reveal the future. Prophecy's accuracy hinges upon the dependency of the one who made the prophecy. Bible prophecy is a vivid description of future events (Acts 15:18). God's Word contains 10,385 predictions *and each one has or will be fulfilled in the minutest detail.* The Bible has proven itself by not failing in even one small point concerning the Lord's First Coming. Prophecy concerning His Second Coming is also presently being fulfilled. Skeptics from the past to the present are increasingly compelled to admit their inability to provide a valid response to the contrary.

PROPHECIES CONCERNING CHRIST

He guards all his bones; not one of them is broken.

PSALM 34:20

The scepter shall not depart from Judah, nor a lawgiver from between his feet, until Shiloh comes; and to Him shall be the obedience of the people.

GENESIS 49:10

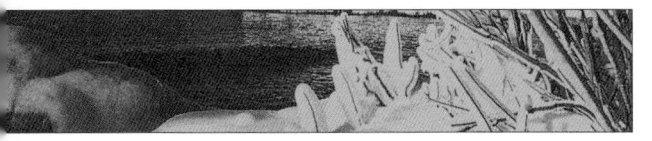

He will be great, and will be called the Son of the Highest; and the Lord God will give Him the throne of His father David. And He will reign over the house of Jacob forever, and of His kingdom there will be no end.

LUKE 1:32, 33

God's Promises of Prophecy

One by one, the prophecies of the Old Testament became reality as a skeptical world awaited the birth and life of their Messiah.

- He would be the seed of a woman (Genesis 3:15)

- He would come through the line of Abraham (Genesis 12:3, 17–19)

- He would be a descendent of Judah (Genesis 49:10)

- He would be crucified (Psalm 22:16)

- He would observe men casting lots for His clothing at His crucifixion (Psalm 34:20)

- He would live again (Job 19:25; Matthew 12:39, 40; 16:3; John 2:19)

Both secular recorded history and the Word of God provide full testimony to the truth that proves each divine prophecy has been fulfilled.

Prophecy Promises
THE ACCURACY OF
THE BIBLE

For prophecy never came by the will of man, but holy men of God spoke as they were moved by the Holy Spirit.

2 PETER 1:21

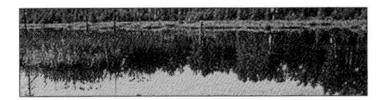

But you, Daniel, shut up the words, and seal the book until the time of the end; many shall run to and fro, and knowledge shall increase.

DANIEL 12:4

For I will take you from among the nations, gather you out of all countries, and bring you into your own land.

EZEKIEL 36:24

God's Promises of Prophecy

The Scriptures were actually statements made through earthly vessels by an all-knowing God. For God, in His omniscience, it is no challenge to describe—in formidable detail—what will happen 100, 1,000, 5,000, even 50,000 years in advance; and—no matter how much time elapses—even the seemingly most insignificant event will happen *precisely as it was prophesied, because God said it.*

For example, there are hundreds of prophecies about Christ's First and Second Coming in the Bible. The law of compound probabilities states that the chance of each one of these being fulfilled is about *one in billions.* Yet, they have all come to pass or are being fulfilled at this very moment in history. God's Word is true. Its far-reaching prophecies have proven the test of time.

THE PALESTINIAN
COVENANT

*Be strong and of good courage, do not fear nor be afraid of them; for the L*ord *your God, He is the One who goes with you. He will not leave you nor forsake you. Then Moses called Joshua and said to him in the sight of all Israel, "Be strong and of good courage, for you must go with this people to the land which the L*ord *has sworn to their fathers to give them, and you shall cause them to inherit it. And the L*ord*, He is the One who goes before you. He will be with you, He will leave you nor forsake you; do not fear nor be dismayed.*

DEUTERONOMY 31:6–8

God's Promises of Prophecy

The Palestinian Covenant
(Deuteronomy 30:1–10) says:

- Israel will be dispersed
among the nations
- Israel will repent and turn to the Lord
- Israel will be gathered
from its dispersion

In this covenant, God promises:

- to bring them to the land
that their fathers possessed
- to prosper them above their fathers
- to restore them spiritually
so that the children of Israel will love
the Lord with all their heart and soul
- to put all manner of curses
on their enemies

The only conditional element on the
people of Israel is the time element.
The actual events *have* and *will* come to
pass. The ultimate fulfillment of God's
promise depends solely upon the
conversion of Israel, when Christ
returns (Romans 11:26).

THE DAVIDIC COVENANT

My covenant I will not break, nor alter the word that has gone out of My lips. Once I have sworn by My holiness; I will not lie to David. His seed shall endure forever, and his throne as the sun before Me; it shall be established forever like the moon, even like the faithful witness in the sky.

PSALM 89:34–37

God's Promises of Prophecy

The *Davidic Covenant* was an unconditional agreement that God made with David. It reaffirmed the Abrahamic Covenant, adding that the blessings would be attached to the lineage of David.

In this covenant, God promises:

- to make David's name great
- to provide a permanent, undisturbed home for Israel
- to establish an eternal kingdom with David and his offspring

Two of these prophecies have been fulfilled, and the third is about to happen, just as the prophets of God said they would come to pass.

Prophecy Promises
THE NEW COVENANT

*Behold, the days are coming, says the LORD, when I will
make a new covenant with the house of Israel and with
the house of Judah—not according to the covenant that I
made with their fathers in the day that I took them by the
hand to lead them out of the land of Egypt, My covenant
which they broke, though I was a husband to them, says
the LORD. But this is the covenant that I will make with the
house of Israel after those days, says the LORD: I will put
My law in their minds, and write it on their hearts; and I
will be their God, and they shall be My people.*

JEREMIAH 31:31–33

God's Promises of Prophecy

God made a New Covenant, again unconditional, with Israel to replace the Mosaic covenant, which the people failed to obey. In this covenant, He promises Israel a profound spiritual restoration.

In this New Covenant, God promises:

- to put His law in their hearts and minds
- to be their God and make them His people
- to forgive their wickedness and remember their sins no more

The moral problem posed by the failure of the Mosaic Covenant will, under the New Covenant, be met by God's own sovereign grace and power. This is offered in the gracious spirit of the earlier Abrahamic Covenant, rather than in the legalistic spirit of the Mosaic Covenant, which it replaces.

DISPENSATIONS—THE "DIVISIONS OF TIME"

So God created man in His own image; in the image of God He created him; male and female He created them.

GENESIS 1:27

Then God spoke to Noah, saying, "Go out of the ark, you and your wife, and your sons, and your sons' wives with you. Bring out with you every living thing of all flesh that is with you: birds and cattle and every creeping thing that creeps on the earth, so that they may abound on the earth, and be fruitful and multiply on the earth."

GENESIS 8:15–17

And Moses went up to God, and the LORD called to him from the mountain, saying, "Thus you shall say to the house of Jacob, and tell the children of Israel: You have seen what I did to the Egyptians, and how I bore you on eagles' wings and brought you to Myself."

EXODUS 19:3, 4

Then I saw an angel coming down from heaven, having the key to the bottomless pit and a great chain in his hand. He laid hold of the dragon, that serpent of old, who is the Devil and Satan, and bound him a thousand years.

REVELATION 20:1, 2

God's Promises of Prophecy

$\mathcal{D}$ispensations are those divisions of time in which mankind responds to a specific revelation of the will of God. There are seven dispensations recorded in Scripture:

1. *Innocence*—Creation to the fall (Genesis 1:27–3:24)

2. *Conscience*—Beginning of civilization to the Flood (Genesis 4:1–8:14)

3. *Human Government*—Exit from the Ark to the Tower of Babel (Genesis 8:15–11:32)

4. *Promise*—Call of Abraham to Egyptian bondage (Genesis 12:1–Exodus 19:2)

5. *Law*—Ten Commandments to the end of the Gospels (Exodus 19:3–Acts 1)

6. *Grace*—Pentecost to end of the Tribulation (Acts 2–Revelation 19:21)

7. *Millennium* (Kingdom)—Imprisonment of Satan to the Great White Throne (Revelation 20:1–22:7)

DISCERNING
TRUE AND FALSE
PROPHETS

*Surely the Lord G*OD *does nothing, unless He reveals
His secret to His servants the prophets.*

AMOS 3:7

The prophets prophesy falsely.

JEREMIAH 5:31

*Give no regard to mediums and familiar spirits; do not
seek after them, to be defiled by them: I am the L*ORD
your God.

LEVITICUS 19:31

*Beware of false prophets, who come to you in sheep's
clothing, but inwardly they are ravenous wolves. . . . Many
will say to Me in that day, "Lord, Lord, have we not
prophesied in Your name, cast out demons in Your name,
and done many wonders in Your name?" And then I will
declare to them, "I never knew you; depart from Me,
you who practice lawlessness!"*

MATTHEW 7:15, 22, 23

God's Promises of Prophecy

A prophet has been shown the order of future events by God Himself. That's the significance of Amos 3:7: *Surely the Lord GOD . . . reveals His secret to His servants the prophets.* Crystal ball-gazers usually *guess* the future, and on occasion they are correct. Others become involved with the spirit world and, when their predictions come true, the results must be attributed to demonic influence. That's why Leviticus 19:31 *(give no regard to mediums and familiar spirits)* is so crucial for Christians who want to know God's final word on the matter.

The Old Testament verification of a prophet included a judgment as to whether he spoke according to the Law (Isaiah 8:20) and whether his prophecy actually came to pass (Deuteronomy 18:22). These criteria have never changed. They remain the basis on which all prophetic utterance is based. Jesus spoke about false prophets in Matthew 7:15, 22, 23.

UNDERSTANDING FUTURE EVENTS

Be diligent to present yourself approved to God, a worker who does not need to be ashamed, rightly dividing the word of truth.

2 TIMOTHY 2:15

Looking for the blessed hope and glorious appearing of our great God and Savior Jesus Christ.

TITUS 2:13

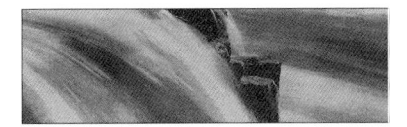

Immediately after the tribulation of those days the sun will be darkened, and the moon will not give its light; the stars will fall from heaven, and the powers of the heavens will be shaken.

MATTHEW 24:29

God's Promises of Prophecy

$\mathcal{T}$o understand and interpret prophetic events with accuracy is a challenge under any circumstance. However, many choose not to spend the time necessary to study the prophetic Scriptures or dig into God's Word, primarily because the task makes tremendous demands on one's spirit and intellect.

Others do not wish to appear to be regarded as *sensationalists.* This is unfortunate, because the event of Christ's return *is* a *sensational* event. The future fact that *the sun will be darkened, and the moon will not give its light; the stars will fall from heaven* (Matthew 24:29) will be a *sensational* moment in history. Christ's return is our *blessed hope* as well as *comforting hope* (1 Thessalonians 4:18). It is also a purifying hope (1 John 3:2, 3) and a hope that will earn one a special crown (2 Timothy 4:7, 8).

ISRAEL AS A NATION

Hear the word of the LORD, O nations, and declare it in the isles afar off, and say, "He who scattered Israel will gather him, and keep him as a shepherd does his flock." For the LORD has redeemed Jacob, and ransomed him from the hand of one stronger than he.

JEREMIAH 31:10, 11

Now learn this parable from the fig tree: When its branch has already become tender and puts forth leaves, you know that summer is near. So you also, when you see all these things, know that it is near—at the doors.

MATTHEW 24:32, 33

And in the days of these kings the God of heaven will set up a kingdom which shall never be destroyed; and the kingdom shall not be left to other people; it shall break in pieces and consume all these kingdoms, and it shall stand forever.

DANIEL 2:44

He will be great, and will be called the Son of the Highest; and the Lord God will give Him the throne of His father David. And He will reign over the house of Jacob forever, and of His kingdom there will be no end.

LUKE 1:32–34

God's Promises of Prophecy

In 1948 Israel became a nation. Matthew 24:32 describes that future—and now fulfilled event—in colorful detail. *That's when the fig tree blossomed.* The fig tree is Israel (Hosea 9:10). The same Word of God that announced the regathering and dispersion of the Jews to the land *God promised them* (Jeremiah 31:10) and Ezekiel's vision of the dry bones in chapter 37, was prophetic of what happened in 1948 when Israel became a nation. This prophecy began with the foretelling of the desert's blossoming "as the rose" (Isaiah 35:1) and the budding of the fig tree, heralding the "generation" that would live to see "all things take place" (Matthew 24:34). We have now seen this prophetic utterance come true.

THE WORLDWIDE CONVERSION OF JEWS

And in that day His feet will stand on the Mount of Olives, which faces Jerusalem on the east. And the Mount of Olives shall be split in two, from east to west, making a very large valley; half of the mountain shall move toward the north and half of it toward the south.

ZECHARIAH 14:4

So the house of Israel shall know that I am the LORD their God from that day forward.

EZEKIEL 39:22

And so all Israel will be saved, as it is written: "The Deliverer will come out of Zion, and He will turn away ungodliness from Jacob; for this is My covenant with them, when I take away their sins."

ROMANS 11:26, 27

When Christ comes and sets His foot upon the Mount of Olives, all the tribes of the earth (the twelve tribes of Israel) will mourn. During the time of the great Tribulation, a total of 144,000 Jews will preach the gospel of the kingdom (Matthew 24:14). Then, when Russia invades the Middle East and God performs one of His greatest miracles on behalf of the Israelites (Ezekiel 39:22), their eyes will be opened.

There is no doubt, according to Scripture, that the Jews will be saved *en masse.* Great as the nation of Israel may be today, her finest and most glorious hour is yet to come as God moves in the hearts of His people once more, and a nationwide conversion of God's people makes the headlines.

And they will fall by the edge of the sword, and be led away captive into all nations. And Jerusalem will be trampled by Gentiles until the times of the Gentiles are fulfilled. And there will be signs in the sun, in the moon, and in the stars; and on the earth distress of nations, with perplexity, the sea and the waves roaring; men's hearts failing them from fear and the expectation of those things which are coming on the earth, for the powers of heaven will be shaken. Then they will see the Son of Man coming in a cloud with power and great glory. Now when these things begin to happen, look up and lift up your heads, because your redemption draws near. . . . So you also when you see these things happening, know that the kingdom of God is near. Assuredly, I say unto you, this generation will by no means pass away till all things take place.

LUKE 21:24–28, 31–32

*T*hroughout history, God has protected His people—the nation of Israel. Scripture states that He will continue to provide for them and that the generation that lives to see all these prophetic events transpire *shall by no means pass away till all things take place.* You and I *are that generation!*

Pope Pius XII, during his Easter sermon at the Vatican in 1957, stated, "There is only one sign that must yet occur and the end-time countdown begins." That sign was the capture of Jerusalem by Jewish armies, which occurred during the Six-Day War fought June 6–10, 1967. Since a generation is usually a time period of forty years (Psalm 95:10), and the generation that lives to see this sign shall not pass from the earth, it is exciting when adding forty years to 1967 that spectacular events could occur in A.D. 2007. While we do not know the day and the hour, we'll know when it's near, even at the door (Matthew 24:33, 36).

"THE TIMES OF THE GENTILES"

And they will fall by the edge of the sword, and be led away captive into all nations. And Jerusalem will be trampled by Gentiles until the times of the Gentiles are fulfilled.

LUKE 21:24

Then you will come from your place out of the far north, you and many peoples with you, all of them riding on horses, a great company, and a mighty army. You will come up against My people of Israel like a cloud, to cover the land. It will be in the latter days that I will bring you against My land, so that the nations may know Me, when I am hallowed in you, O Gog, before their eyes.

EZEKIEL 38:15, 16

Behold, the day of the LORD is coming, and your spoil will be divided in the your midst. For I will gather all the nations to battle against Jerusalem; the city shall be taken, the houses rifled, and the women ravished. Half of the city shall go into captivity, but the remnant of the people shall not be cut off from the city.

ZECHARIAH 14:1, 2

God's Promises of Prophecy

"The times of the Gentiles" simply means Gentile dominion over the Jews and the world, from the period of Jewish captivity—beginning with the Jews' being dispatched against their will to Babylon (Nebuchadnezzar, 536 B.C.) and ending with the third and final battle of the Armageddon campaign and the conclusion of the Tribulation hour.

Events that have occurred since the Six-Day War (1967) prove that Israel's present possession of Jerusalem is temporary. Soon all nations will come against Jerusalem and retake it for a very brief period. At that point, Christ returns to battle the leaders of these nations. Then Jerusalem will be controlled by the Jews forever. The confluence of present events now indicates we are close to that period in history when "the times of the Gentiles" is fulfilled. That final day will come when Messiah appears and destroys the armies of the world. Immediately, the times of the Gentiles will come to an end.

Prophecy Promises

REBUILDING THE TEMPLE IN JERUSALEM

Who opposes and exalts himself above all that is called God or that is worshiped, so that he sits as God in the temple of God, showing himself that he is God.

2 THESSALONIANS 2:4

He was granted power to give breath to the image of the beast, that the image of the beast should both speak and cause as many as would not worship the image of the beast to be killed.

REVELATION 13:15

And from the time that the daily sacrifice is taken away, and the abomination of desolation is set up, there shall be one thousand two hundred and ninety days.

DANIEL 12:11

One day soon, Jerusalem will become the capital of the world, and Yes! at that time the Jews will resume worship in the Temple, again offering sacrifices, as prophesied in God's Word. There could, in fact, be two temples—the one desecrated by the Antichrist where he sits enthroned, calling himself "God" (1 Thessalonians 2:4), and another *after* the seven years of Tribulation mentioned in Ezekiel chapters 40–48.

Many Jews who do not turn to Christ during the Tribulation will return to Temple worship as in Old Testament times—worship that will include the sacrifice of animals. Undoubtedly, permission to build this Temple in Jerusalem will be part of the peace agreement between the final world leader (Antichrist) and the Jews.

THE JEWS RETURN
TO ISRAEL

I will plant them in their land, and no longer shall they be pulled up from the land I have given them, says the LORD your God.

AMOS 9:15

The desolate land shall be tilled instead of lying desolate in the sight of all who pass by. So they will say, "This land that was desolate has become like the garden of Eden; and the wasted, desolate, and ruined cities are now fortified and inhabited." Then the nations which are left all around you shall know that I, the LORD, have rebuilt the ruined places and planted what was desolate. I, the LORD, have spoken it, and I will do it.

EZEKIEL 36:34–36

At that time Jerusalem shall be called The Throne of the LORD, and all the nations shall be gathered to it, to the name of the LORD, to Jerusalem. No more shall they follow the dictates of their evil hearts.

JEREMIAH 3:17

God's Promises of Prophecy

_D_uring the last days, the Jews from around the world will return to Israel. The last group to return home will be from the north—Russia (Jeremiah 3:17, 18)—an event that is already taking place as 820,000 Russian Jews and Gentiles have returned. Matthew 24:31, which describes the introduction to the Millennium, says that when Christ comes to reign for a thousand years, the eighth trumpet sounds, and its blast causes all the elect from the four winds—north, south, east, and west—to return. At that pivotal moment in history, there will be tremendous numbers of Jews from the United States migrating _en masse_ to Israel along with the remainder of Jews from all nations.

All prophetic truth revolves around the Jews, and the Bible reviews their rich history even as it unfolds their future. The future of the world will be determined by the future of the Jews.

THE "ELECT" AND THEIR "SHORTENED DAYS"

And they will fall by the edge of the sword, and be led away captive into all nations. And Jerusalem will be trampled by Gentiles until the times of the Gentiles are fulfilled.

LUKE 21:24

And unless those days were shortened, no flesh would be saved; but for the elect's sake those days will be shortened.

MATTHEW 24:22

Immediately after the tribulation of those days the sun will be darkened, and the moon will not give its light; the stars will fall from heaven, and the powers of the heavens will be shaken.

MATTHEW 24:29

I looked when He opened the sixth seal, and behold, there was a great earthquake; and the sun became black as sackcloth of hair, and the moon became like blood.

REVELATION 6:12

*I*saiah 42:1 speaks of the Jews as God's elect. So does Isaiah 45:4; 65:9; and 65:22. The Scriptures tell us this elect group will flee from Judea (the Holy Land) to the mountains. Because of their history of rejection of Jesus Christ as Messiah (Savior), God, in His foreknowledge, has set up a different schedule for the Jews as a nation than for the Church (the *other* elect). However, it's important to realize that it is the Jews (Israel) whom God has chosen as His wife forever (Jeremiah 3:14).

At the conclusion of the "Time of Jacob's Trouble," Christ returns with an army of believers and judges the nations on the basis of their rejection of Christ and their treatment of Israel (Matthew 25:31–46). All these events will take place in the area of Jerusalem (Luke 21:24).

I personally believe that the shortening of the days cannot mean a lesser period of time. God has presented us with an exact timetable in His word and this cannot change. One half of the seven-year tribulation period totals 1,260 days (Revelation 11:3; 12:6). When doubled, this amounts to 2,520 days. Thus, the "shortening of the days" can only mean a shortening of the daylight hours, lest the blazing effect of the sun destroys all humanity (Revelation 16:8, 9).

THE REVIVAL OF THE ROMAN EMPIRE

You, O king, were watching; and behold, a great image! This great image, whose splendor was excellent, stood before you; and its form was awesome. This image's head was of fine gold, its chest and arms of silver, its belly and thighs of bronze, its legs of iron, its feet partly of iron and partly of clay. You watched while a stone was cut out without hands, which struck the image on its feet of iron and clay, and broke them in pieces. Then the iron, the clay, the bronze, the silver, and the gold were crushed together, and became like chaff from the summer threshing floors; the wind carried them away so that no trace of them was found. And the stone that struck the image became a great mountain and filled the whole earth.

DANIEL 2:31–35

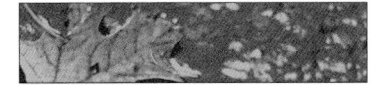

We can reasonably conclude that the dream of Daniel 2 means the Kingdom of God will be established in connection with the Second Coming of our Savior. Just as the image in Nebuchadnezzar's dream contained metals that degraded as they descended from gold to iron and clay, so will the world in which you and I live continue to become apostate, with society governed increasingly by outright militarism as the only vehicle to control the violence that is here and that is yet to come.

When the current revival of the Roman Empire (the European Union) is completed, there will be no other earthly kingdoms to follow. It will be the last empire, one that will continue into the latter days when the Antichrist emerges as the primary figure. Then Christ returns and smashes the final earthly power (Revelation 19:16–20).

Prophecy Promises

THE ONE-WORLD CHURCH

The woman was arrayed in purple and scarlet, and adorned with gold and precious stones and pearls, having in her hand a golden cup full of abominations and the filthiness of her fornication. And on her forehead a name was written: MYSTERY, BABYLON THE GREAT, THE MOTHER OF HARLOTS AND OF THE ABOMINATIONS OF THE EARTH.

REVELATION 17:4, 5

And I saw thrones, and they sat on them, and judgment was committed to them. Then I saw the souls of those who had been beheaded for their witness to Jesus and for the word of God, who had not worshiped the beast or his image, and had not received his mark on their foreheads or on their hands. And they lived and reigned with Christ for a thousand years.

REVELATION 20:4

God's Promises of Prophecy

*A*ll of apostate Christendom
will comprise the one-world church.
All those taken at the Rapture are those
who believed that *all Scripture [was]
given by inspiration of God*
(2 Timothy 3:16), that *holy men of
God spoke as they were moved by the
Holy Spirit* (2 Peter 1:21); they
believed everything the Bible
had to say about Jesus.

However, the churches remaining
after the rapture of the Church will be
those that have chosen to deny this
basic doctrine of Christ. *Who is a liar
but he who denies that Jesus is the
Christ? He is antichrist . . .* (1 John 2:22).
This is one of the sternest warnings in
Scripture to churches and fellowships of
our day—a warning we must heed.

THE RAPTURE OF THE CHURCH

Who also said, "Men of Galilee, why do you stand gazing up into heaven? This same Jesus, who was taken up from you into heaven, will so come in like manner as you saw Him go into heaven."

ACTS 1:11

For the Lord Himself will descend from heaven with a shout, with the voice of an archangel, and with the trumpet of God. And the dead in Christ will rise first. Then we who are alive and remain shall be caught up together with them in the clouds to meet the Lord in the air. And thus we shall always be with the Lord. Therefore comfort one another with these words.

1 THESSALONIANS 4:16–18

Behold, I tell you a mystery: We shall not all sleep, but we shall all be changed—in a moment, in the twinkling of an eye, at the last trumpet. For the trumpet will sound, and the dead will be raised incorruptible, and we shall be changed.

1 CORINTHIANS 15:51, 52

---

*T*he term *rapture* comes from the Latin *rapio* or *rapturo,* which means "a snatching away." The Rapture, then, is that time when the Lord comes in the clouds of glory (Acts 1:11) to take out of this world all those who have died in Christ as well as all believers who are alive at His coming.

The Rapture is the next occurrence on God's calendar and is the literal, visible, and bodily return of Christ in the heavens. He shall return as He left (Acts 1:9–11). This is the great event that will soon take place as the people of God (dead and alive) disappear from the face of the earth, whereupon they immediately meet Christ and are ushered into His presence in the twinkling of an eye.

REVIVAL BEFORE THE RAPTURE

Yes, and all who desire to live godly in Christ Jesus will suffer persecution. But evil men and imposters will grow worse and worse, deceiving and being deceived. But you must continue in the things which you have learned and been assured of, knowing from whom you have learned them.

2 TIMOTHY 3:12–14

And because lawlessness will abound, the love of many will grow cold.

MATTHEW 24:12

I know your works, that you are neither cold nor hot. I could wish you were cold or hot.

REVELATION 3:15

*G*od can do anything at any time. However, the counsel of Scripture does not seem to suggest there will be any great revival before the Rapture. Nevertheless, there *will* be a great revival during the seven-year Tribulation period when 144,000 Jews (Revelation 7:4–8) will circle the globe, preaching the gospel of the kingdom. Their message: *The King is coming!* At that time multitudes will be saved (Revelation 7:9, 14).

The great revival will come *after* the Rapture. However, it is plausible as multitudes see prophecy being fulfilled before their very eyes—and become aware that the Bible is true—that they will want to come to know the Lord.

THE DESTINY OF THE UNBORN DURING THE RAPTURE

But Jesus called them to Him and said, "Let the little children come to Me, and do not forbid them; for of such is the kingdom of God. Assuredly, I say to you, whoever does not receive the kingdom of God as a little child will by no means enter it."

LUKE 18:16, 17

Therefore, as through one man's offense judgment came to all men, resulting in condemnation, even so through one Man's righteous act the free gift came to all men, resulting in justification of life.

ROMANS 5:18

At the time of the Rapture, many Christian mothers will have unborn children living in their wombs. The good news is that all unborn babies will be taken with their mothers—caught up with all believers at the Rapture.

The Bible makes it clear that every fetus within every mother who is taken up in the Rapture will also be taken up. Not only will the ones within their mothers' wombs be caught away, but so will all children who have not yet reached the age of accountability (Luke 18:16). Because of Christ's sacrifice on Calvary's cross, His gift to mankind is freely bestowed upon all until the age of accountability is reached. All children are covered by the blood of Jesus until they know right from wrong. One day God emblazoned Romans 5:18 upon my heart concerning children. Study the text carefully.

THE RAPTURE
BRINGS BLESSING
AND SORROW

*For no other foundation can anyone lay than that which
is laid, which is Jesus Christ. Now if anyone builds on this
foundation with gold, silver, precious stones, wood, hay,
straw, each one's work will become clear; for the Day will
declare it, because it will be revealed by fire; and the fire
will test each one's work, of what sort it is. If anyone's
work which he has built on it endures, he will receive
a reward. If anyone's work is burned, he will suffer loss;
but he himself will be saved, yet so as through fire.*

1 CORINTHIANS 3:11–15

*For what is our hope, or joy, or crown of rejoicing?
Is it not even you in the presence of our Lord Jesus Christ
at His coming? For you are our glory and joy.*

1 THESSALONIANS 2:19, 20

*The twenty-four elders fall down before Him who sits on the
throne and worships Him who lives forever and ever, and
cast their crowns before the throne.*

REVELATION 4:10

Some will be ashamed. For others, it will be the time of ultimate blessing. Think for a moment of those who will stand before the Lord empty-handed. These are men and women who've known the Savior for years but who have no record of godly service. We cannot know all that will be brought to light at that day, but we can be certain that the first question to be asked will be, *Did you bring people to a knowledge of God through His Son, Jesus Christ?*

This is also the last command Jesus presented to us in Acts 1:8, *But you shall receive power when the Holy Spirit has come upon you; and you shall be witnesses to me in Jerusalem, and in all Judea and Samaria, and to the end of the earth.*

Prophecy Promises

UFO'S AND EXTRATERRESTRIAL SIGHTINGS

Then it happened as they continued on and talked, that suddenly a chariot of fire appeared with horses of fire, and separated the two of them; and Elijah went up by a whirlwind into heaven.

2 KINGS 2:11

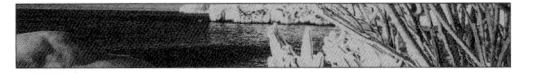

In which you once walked according to the course of this world, according to the prince of the power of the air, the spirit who now works in the sons of disobedience.

EPHESIANS 2:2

For we do not wrestle against flesh and blood, but against principalities, against powers, against the rulers of the darkness of this age, against spiritual hosts of wickedness in the heavenly places. Therefore take up the whole armor of God, that you may be able to withstand in the evil day, and having done all, to stand.

EPHESIANS 6:12, 13

$\mathcal{T}$he Bible teaches that Satan does not reside in hell. He is the prince of the power of the air. That is why we wrestle against the rulers of the darkness of *this* world. As you read this page, millions, perhaps billions, of demonic spirits fill the heavens. Not long ago, four UFO's showed up on screens in Belgium—the first time they were captured on radar. These alien machines and their inhabitants were able to drop thousands of feet in a single second—something that would kill any human . . . *but not angelic beings.*

In Ezekiel 1:16 we read that the wheels (or body) of the prophet's chariot were like beryl. Beryllium (a derivative of beryl) is one of the elements used in our spacecraft today to help withstand the heat and friction of outer-space travel and re-entry to earth. Could it be possible that angels will come and lead us to heaven at the time of the Rapture? Hebrews 1:14 states, *Are they not all ministering spirits sent forth to minister for those who will inherit salvation?*

THE WORLD ECONOMY PRIOR TO THE RAPTURE

They will throw their silver into the streets, and their gold will be like refuse; their silver and their gold will not be able to deliver them in the day of the wrath of the LORD; they will not satisfy their souls, nor fill their stomachs, because it became their stumbling block of iniquity.

EZEKIEL 7:19

Standing at a distance for fear of her torment, saying, "Alas, alas, that great city Babylon, that mighty city! For in one hour your judgment has come." . . . For in one hour such great riches came to nothing. Every shipmaster, all who travel by ship, sailors, and as many as trade on the sea, stood at a distance. . . . And they threw dust on their heads, and cried out, weeping and wailing, and saying, "Alas, alas, that great city, in which all who had ships on the sea became by her wealth! For in one hour is she made desolate."

REVELATION 18:10, 17, 19

*E*veryone today is concerned about the economy. Will it be a bull or a bear market? Will interest rates rise or fall? What will the Fed do next? Another question is also being asked: *Will there be a major economic depression prior to the Rapture?*

This could easily happen soon, because during the Tribulation Hour the economy will become horrendous. It will be so bad that the Prophet Ezekiel said, *They will throw their silver into the streets, and their gold will be like refuse* (Ezekiel 7:19). It will be Babylon revisited. Chaos will abound. The merchants of the earth will weep, because no one will buy their goods, according to Revelation 18:11. All their luxurious baubles will be destroyed. Great riches will come to naught within the span of an hour. This will be the economic fate of our world during the Tribulation.

While this is what we can expect during the Tribulation, we might soon see some recession as we approach that fateful moment because *Jesus is coming soon.*

A PRE-TRIBULATION RAPTURE

*Because you have kept My command to persevere,
I also will keep you from the hour of trial which shall
come upon the whole world, to test those who dwell
on the earth.*

REVELATION 3:10

*Seventy weeks are determined for your people and for your
holy city, to finish the transgression, to make an end of
sins, to make reconciliation for iniquity, to bring in
everlasting righteousness, to seal up vision and prophecy,
and to anoint the Most Holy. Know therefore and
understand, that from the going forth of the command to
restore and build Jerusalem until the Messiah the Prince,
there shall be seven weeks and sixty-two weeks; the street
shall be built again, and the wall, even in troublesome
times. And after the sixty-two weeks Messiah shall be cut
off, but not for Himself; and the people of the prince who is
to come shall destroy the city and the sanctuary. The end
of it shall be with a flood, and till the end of the war
desolations are determined. Then he shall confirm a
covenant with many for one week; but in the middle of the
week he shall bring an end to sacrifice and offering. And
on the wing of abominations shall be one who makes
desolate, even until the consummation which is
determined, is poured out on the desolate.*

DANIEL 9:24–27

God's Promises of Prophecy

Scripture teaches that the Church of Jesus Christ will *not* endure the torment of the Tribulation. For a more thorough understanding of this end-time prophecy, we must spend time studying the amazing book of Daniel. Daniel's seventy weeks are divided into three sections—seven weeks, sixty-two weeks, and one final week. Through logical deduction, we must conclude that since Israel was involved in the sixty-nine weeks of the past, only she could be involved in the final seventieth week—which is the Tribulation hour (See Daniel 9:24). Further, Revelation 3:10 reminds us that God says, *I also will keep you from the hour of trial which shall come upon the whole world.* We also see that the saints are crowned in Revelation 4:10, 11 before the Tribulation period begins in Chapter 6.

Luke 14:14 teaches that believers are recompensed, rewarded, or crowned at the resurrection of the just or the rapture.

Christians often sing the song *This world is not my home, I'm just passing through.* This is good latter-day theology. Christians are not creatures of this earth. Therefore, all who have been ransomed by the blood of the Lord Jesus Christ are kept out of the hour of Tribulation, which is reserved only for the "earth dwellers"—those who have failed to place their allegiance and trust in God through His Son Jesus Christ.

Prophecy Promises

THE MARRIAGE
SUPPER OF THE
LAMB

For I am jealous for you with godly jealousy. For I have betrothed you to one husband, that I may present you as a chaste virgin to Christ.

2 CORINTHIANS 11:2

Let us be glad and rejoice and give Him glory, for the marriage of the Lamb has come, and His wife has made herself ready.

REVELATION 19:7

The next day John saw Jesus coming toward him, and said, "Behold! The Lamb of God who takes away the sin of the world!"

JOHN 1:29

God's Promises of Prophecy

*A*fter all Christians have been judged for service, they are presented in one body (or group) as a *chaste virgin to Christ.* Symbolized as a bride, the Church is then clothed in fine, white linen (See Revelation 19:7, 8).

The Lord Jesus himself is the Bridegroom (Ephesians 5:25–33). The phrase *Marriage of the Lamb* signifies that the Church's union with Christ has been completed. Christ then returns to the earth with His Bride (Revelation 19:7), and the Marriage Supper takes place on earth as all the Old Testament saints and the Tribulation martyrs are resurrected and summoned to this great feast (See Matthew 22:1–14).

The Lamb is Jesus. The great supper that takes place in honor of this Lamb is the One of whom John spoke when he wrote, *Behold! The Lamb of God who takes away the sin of the world!* This Lamb of God is the One Who is worthy to be praised because of His sacrifice for our sins, and the only One worthy to open "the book," the title deed to the earth (Revelation 5:3, 5, 9).

ETERNAL DESTINY OF OLD TESTAMENT AND TRIBULATION SAINTS

After these things I looked, and behold, a door standing open in heaven. And the first voice which I heard was like a trumpet speaking with me, saying, "Come up here, and I will show you things which must take place after this."

REVELATION 4:1

And I saw thrones, and they sat on them, and judgment was committed to them. Then I saw the souls of those who had been beheaded for their witness to Jesus and for the word of God, who had not worshiped the beast or his image, and had not received his mark on their foreheads or on their hands. And they lived and reigned with Christ for a thousand years. But the rest of the dead did not live again until the thousand years were finished. This is the first resurrection. Blessed and holy is he who has part in the first resurrection. Over such the second death has no power, but they shall be priests of God and of Christ, and shall reign with Him a thousand years.

REVELATION 20:4–6

God's Promises of Prophecy

Contrary to the thinking of some, the Old Testament saints cannot be regarded as actual members of the Church. Further, since the Church is evacuated at the Rapture (before the Tribulation begins, Revelation 4:1), we see that the Tribulation saints who are martyred during this horrendous period *also* do not constitute part of the Church. The Church is restricted to that group of believers beginning at Pentecost and brought to fruition at the moment Christ removes the Church to Himself—the Rapture. Both the Old Testament and Tribulation saints *are raised when Christ returns to the earth* so that they may be honored guests at the Marriage Supper of the lamb on earth.

At that momentous feast, modern-day Christians will find themselves seated next to such biblical giants as Daniel, Moses, Isaiah, Jeremiah, and the hundreds of other luminaries of the faith—those who, inspired by God, gave us a prophetic glimpse of God's glory and our own glorious future.

RECOGNIZING LOVED ONES IN HEAVEN

Now after six days Jesus took Peter, James, and John his brother, led them up a high mountain by themselves; and He was transfigured before them. His face shone like the sun, and His clothes became as white as the light.

MATTHEW 17:1, 2

While he was still speaking, behold, a bright cloud overshadowed them; and suddenly a voice came out of the cloud, saying, "This is My beloved Son, in whom I am well pleased. Hear Him!"

MATTHEW 17:5

So it was that the beggar died, and was carried by the angels to Abraham's bosom. The rich man also died and was buried. And being in torment in Hades, he lifted up his eyes and saw Abraham afar off, and Lazarus in his bosom. Then he cried and said, "Father Abraham, have mercy on me, and send Lazarus that he may dip the tip of his finger in water and cool my tongue; for I am tormented in this flame."

LUKE 16:22–24

God's Promises of Prophecy

$\mathcal{T}$he question is often asked, *Will we recognize our loved ones who have gone on before us?* The answer is Yes! Matthew 17:1 literally describes a scene of what it will be like when Jesus returns. Suddenly Moses and Elijah appeared with Jesus. Peter said, "Let's make three tabernacles, Jesus—one for You, one for Moses, and one for Elijah." The disciples did not live in the times of Moses or Elijah, so how could New Testament figures have known that the two men who appeared with Jesus were Moses and Elijah—except by the Spirit of God? Remember, statues and pictures were forbidden under Judaism.

The transfiguration described here is a picture of the Rapture of the Church— when the Lord calls us home. Further proof that we will be able to identify those gone before is found in Luke 16:22–24 where the rich man, Lazarus, and Abraham recognized each other. There is no doubt about it: when we are received into heaven, we can know with confidence that we will recognize the ones we once knew and loved on earth (1 Corinthians 13:12).

"IN THE TWINKLING OF AN EYE"

Behold, I tell you a mystery: We shall not all sleep, but we shall all be changed—in a moment, in the twinkling of an eye, at the last trumpet. For the trumpet will sound, and the dead will be raised incorruptible, and we shall be changed.

1 CORINTHIANS 15:51, 52

For we must all appear before the judgment seat of Christ, that each one may receive the things done in the body, according to what he has done, whether good or bad.

2 CORINTHIANS 5:10

For it is written: "As I live, says the LORD, every knee shall bow to Me, and every tongue shall confess to God." So then each of us shall give account of himself to God.

ROMANS 14:11, 12

A "blink" is calculated to be 11/100ths of a second. A half-blink then becomes the equivalent of the twinkling of an eye. Just as Christ cried out, *Lazarus, come forth* (John 11:43), and immediately Lazarus arose from the dead, so shall the call ring out, *Come up here* (Revelation 4:1), at which time the Church of Jesus Christ will be gone in a glorious flash (1 Corinthians 15:52).

In that "twinkling of an eye," there will be an immediate investigative judgment of the believer's life. At that time, according to Romans 14:12, every one of us shall then give an account of ourselves unto God. The good news is that the iniquity that would have condemned believers to perdition was obliterated when they trusted in the blood of the Savior as payment for their sin. Because of their trust in a living God, believers *shall not come into condemnation; but are passed from death unto life* (John 5:24).

Prophecy Promises

THE "INVESTIGATION" OF BELIEVERS IN HEAVEN

And now, little children, abide in Him, that when He appears, we may have confidence and not be ashamed before Him at His coming.

1 JOHN 2:28

If anyone's work is burned, he will suffer loss; but he himself will be saved, yet so as through fire. Do you not know that you are the temple of God and that the Spirit of God dwells in you?

1 CORINTHIANS 3:15, 16

God's Promises of Prophecy

At the Rapture, all who have placed their trust in Jesus Christ will be carried away and will immediately be ushered into the presence of the Lord. As we're told in Romans 14:10, *We shall all stand before the judgment seat of Christ.* The Bible teaches that we must ALL appear before this judgment seat. Every individual who has been "born again" will be present at this judgment to answer for service rendered or neglected.

At this time, Christians will have a profound understanding of the eternal impact of 1 John 2:28, which pleads for a life of holiness, that we not be ashamed at His coming. Some have argued that Christ will come only for *the perfect.* If this were true, how is it that multitudes of His children could possibly be ashamed at this great meeting? Only an *imperfect* individual will be ashamed before Him, and all Christians will be required to give an account of themselves before Christ—the confident and the ashamed.

Prophecy Promises

CAN SIN KEEP A PERSON OUT OF HEAVEN?

If we say that we have no sin, we deceive ourselves, and the truth is not in us. If we confess our sins, He is faithful and just to forgive us our sins and to cleanse us from all unrighteousness. If we say that we have not sinned, we make Him a liar, and His word is not in us.

1 JOHN 1:8–10

And such were some of you. But you were washed, but you were sanctified, but you were justified in the name of the Lord Jesus and by the Spirit of our God.

1 CORINTHIANS 6:11

For I will be merciful to their unrighteousness, and their sins and their lawless deeds I will remember no more.

HEBREWS 8:12

Those who are ashamed at their meeting with Jesus have done something wrong—but find themselves in the presence of God, nonetheless. They went at the Rapture, but they did not enjoy a glorious entrance. Scripture says there are two ways to enter the presence of God: the *abundant* way (2 Peter 1:11) and the way of fire (1 Corinthians 3:15), the equivalent of entering heaven "by the skin of one's teeth."

If one sin could keep a person out of heaven, no one would make it. Why? Have you ever had a foolish thought? Of course. Who hasn't? Proverbs 24:9 says the *devising of foolishness is sin.* Have you ever had a lack of faith? Romans 14:23 reminds us, *Whatever is not from faith is sin.* We can thank God for His marvelous grace. *But where sin abounded, grace abounded much more* (Romans 5:20). Grace is God's unmerited favor, and, despite our sins, the disobedient among us will be taken in the Rapture and will be present at the Judgment Seat of Christ, but will lose rewards and crowns—having nothing to lay at Jesus' feet.

NEW BELIEVERS
DURING THE
TRIBULATION

And he causes all, both small and great, rich and poor, free and bond, to receive a mark on their right hand or on their foreheads, and that no one may buy or sell except one who has the mark or the name of the beast, or the number of his name.

REVELATION 13:16, 17

When the Son of Man comes in His glory, and all the holy angels with Him, then He will sit on the throne of His glory. All the nations will be gathered before Him, and He will separate them one from another, as a shepherd divides his sheep from the goats. And He will set the sheep on His right hand, but the goats on the left. Then the King will say to those on His right hand, "Come, you blessed of My Father, inherit the kingdom prepared for you from the foundation of the world." . . . Then He will also say to those on the left hand, "Depart from Me, you cursed, into the everlasting fire prepared for the devil and his angels."

MATTHEW 25:31–34, 41

*R*evelation 20:4 makes it clear that individuals who do not receive the mark of the beast will be killed. This is the "666" mark, without which no person will be able to buy or sell. However, Scripture hints at an alternative for those who come to know the Lord during this horrendous Tribulation hour. In Matthew 24:16 we read, *Then let those who are in Judea flee to the mountains.* Perhaps these new believers will grow their own crops and be able to keep their lives on course by mutual cooperation with other Christians.

We do know that not all will die as believers (See Matthew 25:31–46), for when Christ returns and judges the nations, there will be millions of Christians still alive, even though they rejected the mark of the beast. Although details are not clear, it is certain that God will provide a way for these believers in Christ to live their lives in relative security during the Tribulation without accepting the mark.

THE TRIBULATION— THE WORST EVENT IN HISTORY

Alas! For that day is great, so that none is like it; and it is the time of Jacob's trouble, but he shall be saved out of it.

JEREMIAH 30:7

There shall be a time of trouble, such as never was since there was a nation, even to that time. And at that time your people shall be delivered, every one who is found written in the book.

DANIEL 12:1

A day of darkness and gloominess, a day of clouds and thick darkness, like the morning clouds spread over the mountains. A people come, great and strong, the like of whom has never been; nor will there ever be any such after them, even for many successive generations.

JOEL 2:2

*T*here will be nothing in past history to compare to the terror of the Tribulation. The trauma of this terrible hour has been prophesied by such Old Testament saints as Jeremiah, Daniel, Joel, and in the words of Jesus Himself when He said in Matthew 24:21, *For then there will be great tribulation, such as has not been since the beginning of the world until this time, no, nor ever shall be.*

It will be a time of great darkness. The Antichrist will appear center stage— pretending to be God, yet seducing the nations to believe he is the leader they all have been anticipating. Russia will invade Israel from the north—a time when Israel is at peace, all ending at the third and final battle of the Armageddon campaign and the return of Jesus Christ to earth. Each prophet throughout history has essentially said the same thing—that the Tribulation cannot be compared to anything we've ever known, nor will there be anything in the future that will remotely measure up to its horrors.

Prophecy Promises

THE POSSIBILITY OF NUCLEAR WAR DURING THE TRIBULATION

A fire goes before Him, and burns up His enemies round about.

PSALM 97:3

I will send fire on Magog.

EZEKIEL 39:6

The first angel sounded: And hail and fire followed mingled with blood, and they were thrown to the earth. And a third of the trees were burned up, and all green grass was burned up.

REVELATION 8:7

By these three plagues was a third of mankind killed—by the fire and the smoke and the brimstone which came out of their mouths.

REVELATION 9:18

The Scripture teaches there will be an all encompassing nuclear war during the Tribulation, with Revelation 9:18 describing the effects of such a nuclear blast. Scripture after Scripture reveals a judgment of fire taking place upon earth during this "Time of Jacob's Trouble." Joel 2:30 states, *I will show wonders in the heavens and in the earth: blood and fire and pillars of smoke.* We read in Zephaniah 1:18, *The whole land shall be devoured by the fire of His jealousy.*

There is no escaping the reality that the Bible is describing the devastating, worldwide effects of nuclear war. Perhaps Malachi 4:1 says it most convincingly, *For behold, the day is coming, burning like an oven.* The Tribulation will be horrific enough with the Antichrist running—and ruining— the show. But nothing will compare to the horrors of this biblically prophesied nuclear holocaust. The good news, however, is that those who put their trust in Christ will already be called home and will not endure the pain of this terrible moment in history.

WORDS THAT BEST
DESCRIBE THE
TRIBULATION

Alas! For that day is great, so that none is like it; and it is the time of Jacob's trouble, but he shall be saved out of it.

JEREMIAH 30:7

A day of darkness and gloominess, a day of clouds and thick darkness, like the morning clouds spread over the mountains. A people come, great and strong, the like of whom has never been; nor will there ever be any such after them, even for many successive generations.

JOEL 2:2

The earth shall reel to and fro like a drunkard, and shall totter like a hut; its transgression shall be heavy upon it, and it will fall, and not rise again.

ISAIAH 24:20

Saying with a loud voice, "Fear God and give glory to Him, for the hour of His judgment has come; and worship Him who made heaven and earth, the sea and springs of water."

REVELATION 14:7

God's Promises of Prophecy

The Word of God describes the great Tribulation in specific terms:

- *Punishment*—Isaiah 24:20–23
- *Indignation*—Isaiah 26:20, 21
  - *Trouble*—Jeremiah 30:7
  - *Destruction*—Joel 1:15
  - *Darkness*—Joel 2:2
  - *Trials*—Revelation 3:10
- *Wrath*—Revelation 6:16, 17; 1 Thessalonians 1:10; 5:9
- *Judgment*—Revelation 14:7; 19:2

We are closer than many think to this terrible moment in history. Increasingly "end-time technology" is being offered to an unsuspecting public: advances in satellite tracking systems, bio-engineering, global communications, video imaging, bio-mouse "fingerprint" scanners, and skin implants or "invisible tattoos." The stage for the Tribulation is now set . . . and, in the words of Scripture, the hour or punishment, indignation, trouble, destruction, darkness, trials, wrath, and judgment is near.

WHAT WILL TRIGGER THE GREAT TRIBULATION?

For when they say, "Peace and safety!" then sudden
destruction comes upon them, as labor pains upon
a pregnant woman. And they shall not escape.

1 THESSALONIANS 5:3

The people of the prince who is to come shall destroy the
city and the sanctuary. The end of it shall be with
a flood, and till the end of the war desolations are
determined. Then he shall confirm a covenant with many
for one week; but in the middle of the week he shall bring
an end to sacrifice and offering. And on the wing of
abominations shall be one who makes desolate, even until
the consummation, which is determined, is poured out on
the desolate.

DANIEL 9:26

You will say, "I will go up against a land of unwalled
villages; I will go to a peaceful people, who dwell safely,
all of them dwelling without walls, and having neither bars
nor gates."

EZEKIEL 38:11

The Tribulation Hour will not *just happen*. It will be set in motion when the Antichrist arises from the revived Roman Empire (the European Union, or EU) and starts his peace negotiations with the nations. The night the contract is signed is the beginning of the Tribulation hour—the seven-year period of trouble and woe. One can begin the countdown from the moment that peace agreement is put in contract form—a total of 2,520 days until Christ's return to earth. While we will not know the day or the hour for the "Rapture," we will know the day for the "Revelation"—Christ's return to earth.

The appearance of the Antichrist is well documented in Scripture, with perhaps the most forceful passage found in 1 Thessalonians 2:3 where it states that he is *that man of sin.* The Antichrist is the embodiment of lawlessness, seduction, and power, a beast, a king of fierce countenance, the wicked one. He will rule for a season, but the final victory belongs to the Lord!

DANIEL'S SEVENTIETH WEEK

The first was like a lion, and had eagle's wings. I watched till its wings were plucked off; and it was lifted up from the earth and made to stand on two feet like a man, and a man's heart was given to it. And suddenly another beast, a second, like a bear. It was raised up on one side, and had three ribs in its mouth between its teeth. And they said thus to it: "Arise, devour much flesh!" After this I looked, and there was another, like a leopard, which had on its back four wings of a bird. The beast also had four heads, and dominion was given to it. After this I saw in the night visions, and behold, a fourth beast, dreadful and terrible, and exceedingly strong. It had huge iron teeth; it was devouring, breaking in pieces, and trampling the residue with its feet. It was different from all the beasts that were before it, and it had ten horns.

DANIEL 7:4–7

And the ten horns are ten kings who shall arise from this kingdom. And another shall rise after them; He shall be different from the first ones, and shall subdue three kings. He shall speak pompous words against the Most High, shall persecute the saints of the Most High, and intend to change times and law. Then the saints shall be given into his hand for a time and times and half a time.

DANIEL 7:24, 25

God's Promises of Prophecy

Skeptics do not appreciate the predictions of the prophet Daniel. His outline of the future is far too accurate and compelling. By interpreting King Nebuchadnezzar's dream as a young man, Daniel gave Christians throughout history what has become known as the "ABC's of Prophecy." Near the end of his life, Daniel was visited by the angel Gabriel, at which time he was given a timetable of coming events that would especially affect the nation of Israel. This is known as the vision of *Seventy Weeks*—the backbone of biblical prophecy.

In this vision Daniel saw the major world empires represented by four beasts—a lion, bear, leopard, and the fourth so grotesque in appearance that it goes unnamed, except to say that it was *dreadful and terrible, and exceedingly strong*. This fourth beast represents the revived Roman Empire or the present-day European Union—the only prophecy in Daniel's dream yet to be totally fulfilled. This represents the seventieth week of Daniel when the Antichrist breaks all his pledges to Israel and an era of unthinkable persecution breaks out—especially for the Jews. We are now waiting for the seventieth week, that period of time that is about to usher in what the Bible calls the "Time of Jacob's Trouble."

Prophecy Promises

"THE DAY OF THE LORD"

For you yourselves know perfectly that the day of the Lord so comes as a thief in the night. For when they say, "Peace and safety!" then sudden destruction comes upon them, as labor pains upon a pregnant woman. And they shall not escape. But you, brethren, are not in darkness, so that this Day should overtake you as a thief.

1 THESSALONIANS 5:2–4

But the day of the Lord will come as a thief in the night, in which the heavens will pass away with a great noise, and the elements will melt with fervent heat; both the earth and the works that are in it will be burned up. Therefore, since all these things will be dissolved, what manner of persons ought you to be in holy conduct and godliness, looking for and hastening the coming of the day of God, because of which the heavens will be dissolved, being on fire, and the elements will melt with fervent heat?

2 PETER 3:10–12

The Day of the Lord begins as the period of the Great Tribulation commences and continues throughout the 1,000-year reign of Christ, because the purification of the world by fire later is still called the day of the Lord (2 Peter 3:10). Some suggest that this is the Rapture, but this cannot be justified by Scripture. This is why the Bible states that the "day of the Lord" comes as *a thief in the night.* Believers awaiting the Rapture will not be surprised or overtaken by the "thief in the night" event (1 Thessalonians 5:4, 5). The "day of the Lord" event seven years later will seem like a time of peace, contentment, and safety for millions. Then suddenly, and without warning, all hell will break loose on earth. Those who do not know the Savior will have no means of escape from the ravages of an Antichrist-run world. The terrible time of doom will have already begun . . . and will continue for a thousand years.

ONE WILL BE TAKEN, ONE LEFT BEHIND

Then two men will be in the field: one will be taken and the other left. Two women will be grinding at the mill: one will be taken and the other left.

MATTHEW 24:40, 41

So I looked, and behold a pale horse. And the name of him who sat on it was Death, and Hades followed with him. And power was given to them over a fourth of the earth, to kill with sword, with hunger, with death, and by the beasts of the earth.

REVELATION 6:8

By these three plagues a third of mankind was killed—by the fire and the smoke and the brimstone which came out of their mouths. **REVELATION 9:18**

*O*nly 2 percent of the population of the world knows Jesus Christ as personal Savior. This leaves 98 percent who do not. Therefore, since we could not have 50 percent of the population taken at the Rapture (one taken, one left), Matthew 24:40 cannot refer to the Rapture itself. However, it does tie in with judgment. The "pale horse" plague and his rider named "death" referred to in Revelation 6:8 is quite possibly a picture of the AIDS virus, among others. If one fourth of the world's population of six billion is destroyed in this manner— 1,500,000,000 people—that would leave 4,500,000,000.

By the time we arrive at Revelation 9:18, nuclear war has already begun: *By these three plagues a third of mankind was killed—by the fire and the smoke and the brimstone which came out of their mouths.* When we remove another one third or 1,500,000,000 of the remaining 4,500,000,000, we end up with 3 billion. Then only one half of the population of the planet remains—one out of two, as we read in Matthew 24:40, *one will be taken and the other left.*

Prophecy Promises

THE "DRY BONES" OF EZEKIEL

Then He said to me, "Son of man, these bones are the whole house of Israel. They indeed say, 'Our bones are dry, our hope is lost, and we ourselves are cut off!' Therefore prophesy and say to them, 'Thus says the Lord GOD: "Behold, O My people, I will open your graves and cause you to come up from your graves, and bring you into the land of Israel. Then you shall know that I am the LORD, when I have opened your graves, O My people, and brought you up from your graves. I will put My Spirit in you, and you shall live, and I will place you in your own land. Then you shall know that I, the LORD, have spoken it and performed it," says the LORD.' "

EZEKIEL 37:11–14

A vivid description of the scattering and return of Israel is given by the prophet Ezekiel in his vision of the valley of dry bones. He is transported to a great valley filled with dry, bleached bones that have been exposed to the elements and the ravages of time. The prophet was asked if those bones could live and was further instructed to prophesy about their significance. While he was speaking, the bones joined together, the skeletons were covered with flesh, and the organs began to pulsate with life. The once dry bones now become living beings, standing to their feet at attention as a great army.

These bones then return to their own land, the miraculous historical event that occurred May 14, 1948. This prophecy is identical to "the budding" of the fig tree in Matthew 24:32, and the fig tree is Israel (Hosea 9:10; Joel 1:7).

THE IDENTITY OF THE ANTICHRIST

Little children, it is the last hour; and as you have heard that the Antichrist is coming, even now many antichrists have come, by which we know that it is the last hour.

1 JOHN 2:18

For the mystery of lawlessness is already at work; only He who now restrains will do so until He is taken out of the way. And then the lawless one will be revealed, whom the Lord will consume with the breath of His mouth and destroy with the brightness of His coming.

2 THESSALONIANS 2:7, 8

Let no one deceive you by any means; for that Day will not come unless the falling away comes first, and the man of sin is revealed, the son of perdition, who opposes and exalts himself above all that is called God or that is worshiped, so that he sits as God in the temple of God, showing himself that he is God.

2 THESSALONIANS 2:3, 4

*W*ill Christians know the identity of the Antichrist prior to the Rapture? No. Scripture clearly teaches that the Rapture occurs *before* "that man of sin" makes his diabolic appearance or is *revealed* (2 Thessalonians 2:3, 4, 8). Since the bodies of Christians are temples of the Holy Spirit, we are the hinderers who hold back the Antichrist's appearing. Once we are taken out of the way, the Antichrist *is revealed.* I repeat, only after the hinderer—the Holy Spirit, who lives in the hearts of believers—is removed, will the Church discover the identity of the Antichrist. Therefore, only those who are left behind become acquainted with this monstrous dictator who ushers in the Tribulation hour.

THE APPEARANCE OF
THE ANTICHRIST

Then I stood on the sand of the sea. And I saw a beast rising up out of the sea, having seven heads and ten horns, and on his horns ten crowns, and on his heads a blasphemous name.

REVELATION 13:1

Then he shall confirm a covenant with many for one week; but in the middle of the week he shall bring an end to sacrifice and offering. And on the wing of abominations shall be one who makes desolate, even until the consummation, which is determined, is poured out on the desolate.

DANIEL 9:27

And in the latter time of their kingdom, when the transgressors have reached their fullness, a king shall arise, having fierce features who understands sinister schemes.

DANIEL 8:23

The Antichrist is undoubtedly alive at this moment—an observation largely because of what we're seeing with the emergence of the European Union (revived Roman Empire). The Bible teaches that the Antichrist—the final world ruler—will come out of an alignment of nations such as the EU (European Union). (See Daniel 2, 7; Revelation 13:1). The EU has risen rapidly and plays a most important part in latter-day predictions.

For 2,500 years, there was no nation called Israel—until 1948, when she raised up the six-pointed star of David. From 1948 until 1979 Israel was in a constant state of military preparedness for war. Then, on Monday, March 26, 1979, Israel and Egypt signed their historic pact. But *that was not the contract spoken of in Daniel 9:27.* For this reason: the agreement must be signed *in the presence of the western leader* [the Antichrist] and with *many nations.* Given the accelerated speed of end-time events in our era, there is little question that the Antichrist is alive.

Prophecy Promises

THE PEACEFUL "FIRST HALF" OF THE TRIBULATION

And in his place shall arise a vile person, to whom they will not give the honor of royalty; but he shall come in peaceably, and seize the kingdom by intrigue.

DANIEL 11:21

For when they say, "Peace and safety!" then sudden destruction comes upon them, as labor pains upon a pregnant woman. And they shall not escape.

1 THESSALONIANS 5:3

But in their place he shall honor a god of fortresses; and a god which his fathers did not know he shall honor with gold and silver, with precious stones and pleasant things.

DANIEL 11:38

𝒯he first half of the seven-year Tribulation will manifest all the attributes of stability. The leader (Antichrist) who comes out of the revived Roman Empire will portray himself as a man of peace (Daniel 11:21), but he actually honors the *God of fortresses* [armed forces]. He comes to power on a platform of peace. So skilled and manipulative is he that he persuades the nations to sign a peace agreement for seven years and also creates a negotiable plan for Israel's third temple. Politically, he cannot show his colors too soon. That's why the Scripture prophesies that in the middle of the seven years this so-called man of peace breaks his contract and causes the temple sacrifices and oblations to cease.

The Antichrist dupes the world as a man who has campaigned on a platform of peace, but, because he breaks that agreement of peace, shows the world who he really is: *a man of war.* He is one of the key players in the Mid-East war (Daniel 11:40–45), as well as in the third and final battle of the Armageddon campaign. At this point he and his armies attempt to stop the setting up of Christ's kingdom (Psalm 2:1–6; Revelation 19:19).

THE MARK OF
THE BEAST

He causes all, both small and great, rich and poor, free and slave, to receive a mark on their right hand or on their foreheads, and that no one may buy or sell except one who has the mark or the name of the beast, or the number of his name. Here is wisdom. Let him who has understanding calculate the number of the beast, for it is the number of a man: His number is 666.

REVELATION 13:16–18

So the first went and poured out his bowl upon the earth, and a foul and loathsome sore came upon the men who had the mark of the beast and those who worshiped his image.

REVELATION 16:2

Let no one deceive you by any means; for that Day will not come unless the falling away comes first, and the man of sin is revealed, the son of perdition.

2 THESSALONIANS 2:3

The rise of the Antichrist—the Beast—is the most significant political event during the Tribulation period. He is described in detail by John in Revelation 13. In the Old Testament, the prophet Daniel spoke of him as the "little horn" whose power would reach its zenith for three and one half years (half the time of the Tribulation).

Revelation 13:18 reminds us, *Let him who has understanding calculate the number of the beast, for it is the number of a man: His number is 666.* The number "666" is the number of the Beast. The Beast is also described in Scripture as *a king . . . having fierce features* (Daniel 8:23); *the prince that shall come* (Daniel 9:26); *the son of perdition* (2 Thessalonians 2:3); and *the lawless one* (2 Thessalonians 2:8). Without the mark of the beast, no individual during the Tribulation period will be able to buy or sell.

THE POWER OF THE WORLD RELIGIOUS LEADER

And he exercises all the authority of the first beast in his presence, and causes the earth and those who dwell in it to worship the first beast, whose deadly wound was healed. He performs great signs, so that he even makes fire come down from heaven on the earth in the sight of men. And he deceives those who dwell on the earth by those signs which he was granted to do in the sight of the beast, telling those who dwell on the earth to make an image to the beast who was wounded by the sword and lived. He was granted power to give breath to the image of the beast, that the image of the beast should both speak and cause as many as would not worship the image of the beast to be killed.

REVELATION 13:12–15

$\mathcal{B}$ecause of his enormous popularity, the Antichrist persuades the world to see him as the god they've longingly anticipated. The False Prophet makes an image of the beast and commands that people worship the Antichrist (the substitute for Christ) globally. Not only does he perform miracles to enhance his acceptance by a gullible world (see Revelation 13:14), but he actually makes the image of the beast come to life and speak (see Revelation 13:15).

We must take this possibility seriously in light of the advancement of today's technology. We have talking robots and talking computers. Once again, we are compelled to conclude that the Bible sees these events eons before they take place. The stage is set. The Antichrist and the False Prophet are undoubtedly alive and positioning themselves for world leadership.

Prophecy Promises

THE "THREE HEAVENS"

I know a man in Christ who fourteen years ago—whether in the body I do not know, or whether out of the body I do not know, God knows—such a one was caught up to the third heaven. And I know such a man—whether in the body or out of the body I do not know, God knows.

2 CORINTHIANS 12:2, 3

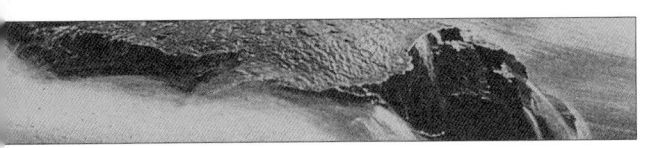

*J*esus spoke about two places in eternity—heaven and hell. John 14:1–6 reminds us that death is not a sad ending for the believer, but, in fact, a glorious beginning. Heaven is so real that God provides some amazing details concerning its location. His Word speaks of three heavens: The first heaven consists of the atmosphere, troposphere, stratosphere, mesosphere, ionosphere, and exosphere and reaches upwards into the first 600 miles of space; the second heaven reaches from 600 miles upward to billions of light years into space; the third heaven is God's holy hemisphere (2 Corinthians 12:2, 3).

Heaven is upward and in the north (Psalm 48:2; Isaiah 14:13). Skeptics now must deal with the scientific data being collected by astronomers who tell us there is an opening in the universe to get *to* this third heaven. It is in the north, in the constellation of "Swan." This should come as no surprise to the believer who remembers the words of Job, *He stretches out the north over empty space* (Job 26:7). Again, the Word of God has clearly prophesied what will surely come to pass.

HEAVENS AND EARTH, NEW AND OLD

In which you once walked according to the course of this world, according to the prince of the power of the air, the spirit who now works in the sons of disobedience.

EPHESIANS 2:2

For behold, I create new heavens and a new earth: and the former shall not be remembered or come to mind.

ISAIAH 65:17

And he showed me a pure river of water of life, clear as crystal, proceeding from the throne of God and of the Lamb. In the middle of its street, and on either side of the river, was the tree of life, which bore twelve fruits, each tree yielding its fruit every month. The leaves of the tree were for the healing of the nations.

REVELATION 22:1, 2

God's Promises of Prophecy

The present earth and heaven will be
purified after the Great White Throne
Judgment by something akin to a
nuclear blast (2 Peter 3:10, 11). One of
the heavens referred to in this passage is
at least the first heaven, the atmosphere
extending upward to the exosphere and
the first 600 miles into space, which has
been defiled because of Satan and his
wickedness (Ephesians 2:2). It's also
possible that the destruction of the
second heaven—from which Satan
makes his accusations against the
brethren to God, who dwells in the third
heaven—takes place at this time.

This happens as a prelude to refining the
old world (Isaiah 65:17). God then
presents us with a new heaven and a new
earth, thus bringing to prophetic fulfillment
what is written in Revelation 21:1,
*Now I saw a new heaven and a new
earth, for the first heaven and the first
earth had passed away. Also there was no
more sea.* We then dwell on this purified
earth forever (Isaiah 45:17; Luke 1:33;
Ephesians 3:21; Revelation 11:15).

THE FINAL DESTINY
OF THE ANTICHRIST

Then the beast was captured, and with him the false prophet who worked signs in his presence, by which he deceived those who received the mark of the beast and those who worshiped his image. These two were cast alive into the lake of fire burning with brimstone.

REVELATION 19:20, 21

And the smoke of their torment ascends forever and ever; and they have no rest day nor night, who worship the beast and his image, and whoever receives the mark of his name.

REVELATION 14:11

The Antichrist—the Beast—and the false prophet are *both cast alive into the lake of fire burning with brimstone* (Revelation 19:20). People often wonder, *Can this be literal fire? Would not the bodies disintegrate in the intense heat?* Let's hold that question for a moment. A thousand years later, Satan is cast into that same place: *The devil, who deceived them, was cast into the lake of fire and brimstone where the beast and the false prophet are* (Revelation 20:10). When the devil is cast into the lake of fire, the beast and the false prophet are still intact—a thousand years later. So they obviously survived the flames, but the smoke of their torment endured *forever and ever* (Revelation 14:11). In Matthew 25:46 we read: *And these will go away into everlasting punishment, but the righteous into eternal life.* In this text the identical Greek word is used for both everlasting punishment and life eternal. The one must be as long as the other. Therefore, both heaven and hell are forever.

GOD'S PROPHETIC CLOCK

When the Son of Man comes in His glory, and all the holy angels with Him, then He will sit on the throne of His glory. All the nations will be gathered before Him, and He will separate them one from another, as a shepherd divides his sheep from the goats. And He will set the sheep on His right hand, but the goats on the left.

MATTHEW 25:31–33

Now when the thousand years have expired, Satan will be released from his prison and will go out to deceive the nations which are in the four corners of the earth, Gog and Magog, to gather them together to battle, whose number is as the sand of the sea. And they went up on the breadth of the earth and surrounded the camp of the saints and the beloved city. And fire came down from God out of heaven and devoured them.

REVELATION 20:7–9

*O*ne week of years (Daniel's seventieth week) remains to be fulfilled when the Age of Grace is over and the Church is raptured. At this time, Israel will again become the object of God's special dealing, and the final seven years of Daniel's vision will be counted off during the most terrible time the world has ever seen—the Tribulation period.

The prophetic clock ticks on during the seven years as God's plan for the ages continues—ending in the Battle of Armageddon and the return of Christ when He defeats all opposing armies. Satan is then bound for a thousand years. Christ judges the nations and the rebels are punished (Matthew 25:31–46). Next is the millennial or the thousand-year reign of Christ, after which Satan is set free for a brief period and later is cast into a lake of fire. The prophetic clock finally winds down completely with the emergence of the Great White Throne Judgment, the purification of the old earth and heavens, and the creation of the new.

THE SEQUENCE OF TRIBULATION EVENTS

Then I stood on the sand of the sea. And I saw a beast rising up out of the sea, having seven heads and ten horns, and on his horns ten crowns, and on his heads a blasphemous name.

REVELATION 13:1

For God has put it into their hearts to fulfil His purpose, to be of one mind, and to give their kingdom to the beast, until the words of God are fulfilled.

REVELATION 17:17

Then the beast was captured, and with him the false prophet who worked signs in his presence by which he deceived those who received the mark of the beast and those who worshiped his image. These two were cast alive into the lake of fire burning with brimstone.

REVELATION 19:20, 21

There are eight definitive time periods during the Tribulation:

1. The Tribulation begins with the rise of the Antichrist (out of the European Union—the EU) as the leader of a global confederacy. (Daniel 7:23; Revelation 13:7).

2. He signs a seven-year peace contract with Israel (Daniel 9:27).

3. After forty-two months, Antichrist breaks the contract (Daniel 9:27).

4. Russia invades Israel from the north at a time when Israel is at rest or peace (Ezekiel 38:11).

5. Antichrist attempts to destroy God's people, the Jews (Revelation 12:13).

6. He destroys the world church that helped bring him to power (Revelation 17:16,17).

7. He proclaims himself as God (2 Thessalonians 2:4–11).

8. He himself is destroyed at Armageddon (Revelation 19) and is cast into the lake of fire (Revelation 19:20).

THE BATTLE OF ARMAGEDDON

And they gathered them together to the place called in Hebrew, Armageddon.

REVELATION 16:16

I will also gather all nations, and bring them down to the Valley of Jehoshaphat; and I will enter into judgment with them there on account of My people, My heritage Israel, whom they have scattered among the nations; they have also divided up My land.

JOEL 3:2

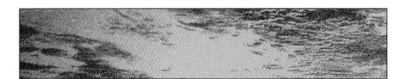

And in that Day his feet will stand on the Mount of Olives, which faces Jerusalem on the east. And the Mount of Olives shall be split in two, from east to west, making a very large valley; half of the mountain shall move toward the north and half of it toward the south.

ZECHARIAH 14:4

The third phase of the battle of Armageddon is the last move against the Lord Jesus Christ by all the world leaders, centered in the Middle East. The valley of Megiddo is where the troops gather for the Battle of Armageddon. *Armageddon* is a wordplay on the Greek, found in Revelation 16:16, and promises to be the most horrendous series of battles the world has ever seen.

The armies of the world gather at *Armageddon* and quickly move from that central location to the *valley of Jehoshaphat* (Zechariah 14:4) to await Christ's appearing as He descends from the M*ount of Olives*. At that moment, every soldier from every nation who remains will attack Jerusalem in an attempt to prevent Christ from setting up His world headquarters there. This is when Christ puts down all earth's forces and creates a thousand years of Utopia on earth.

WORLD ARMIES GATHER IN ISRAEL FOR THE FINAL BATTLE

The LORD did not set His love on you nor choose you because you were more in number than any other people, for you were the least of all peoples, but because the LORD loves you, and because He would keep the oath which He swore to your fathers, the LORD has brought you out with a mighty hand, and redeemed you from the house of bondage, from the hand of Pharaoh king of Egypt.

DEUTERONOMY 7:7, 8

Then they will deliver you up to tribulation and kill you, and you will be hated by all nations for My name's sake.

MATTHEW 24:9

Now when the dragon saw that he had been cast to the earth, he persecuted the woman who gave birth to the male Child.

REVELATION 12:13

---

*W*hy will the world's armies be gathered in Israel? Because anti-Semitism will reign to the bitter end. The world has always hated the Jews, a fact witnessed by the almost unbelievable treatment they have received for thousands of years. Yet, God continues to love the Jews in a special way (Deuteronomy 7:7, 8). John writes that *He came unto His own.* When God wanted to give mankind the law—the commandments—He chose the Jews (Read Romans 9:1–5). They are *His* people, even though few other nations choose to be intimately associated with them—a number that is steadily increasing.

One needs read only a small portion of history to recognize that Satan, too, hates the Jews and has done his best to eradicate them from the face of the earth. Why? Because the Jews were responsible for giving us the Savior and the Word of God. When the nations gather against Israel for the final battle, this will be Satan's last feeble attempt to destroy the Jews—but he will not be successful. He will go down in ignominious defeat. Psalm 122:6 states, *Pray for the peace of Jerusalem: may they prosper who love you.*

Prophecy Promises

THE DAY AND HOUR OF CHRIST'S RETURN TO EARTH

Know therefore and understand, that from the going forth of the command to restore and build Jerusalem until Messiah the Prince, there shall be seven weeks and sixty-two weeks; the street shall be built again, and the wall, even in troublesome times. And after sixty-two weeks Messiah shall be cut off, but not for Himself; and the people of the prince who is to come shall destroy the city and the sanctuary. The end of it shall be with a flood, and till the end of the war desolations are determined. Then he shall confirm a covenant with many for one week; but in the middle of the week he shall bring an end to sacrifice and offering. And on the wing of abominations shall be the one who makes desolate, even until the consummation, which is determined, is poured out on the desolate.

DANIEL 9:25–27

*C*an anyone know the day and the hour of the "Revelation"—the day when the Lord Jesus returns to earth? Yes. When the Antichrist persuades Israel to sign his international peace contract (Daniel 9:27), one can begin marking off the days on the calendar. The Battle of Armageddon and Christ's return to earth will be exactly 2,520 days from the date of this signing. The Revelation, however, is *not* the Rapture. No one knows the day or the hour for that *great escape*—when we will meet Jesus in the clouds. But we *can* know the day and hour of the Revelation— when Jesus returns with His saints. Jude 14 says, *The Lord comes with ten thousands of His saints.* That is you and I. Then we rule and reign with Christ for 1,000 years (Revelation 20:4).

THE CLOSING SCENES
OF THE TRIBULATION

When the Son of Man comes in His glory, and all the holy angels with Him, then He will sit on the throne of His glory. All the nations will be gathered before Him, and He will separate them one from another, as a shepherd divides his sheep from the goats. And He will set the sheep on His right hand, but the goats on the left. Then the King will say to those on His right hand, "Come, you blessed of My Father, inherit the kingdom prepared for you from the foundation of the world."

MATTHEW 25:31–34

And many of those who sleep in the dust of the earth shall awake, some to everlasting life, some to shame and everlasting contempt.

DANIEL 12:2

And I saw thrones, and they sat on them, and judgment was committed to them. Then I saw the souls of those who had been beheaded for their witness to Jesus and for the word of God, who had not worshiped the beast or his image, and had not received his mark on their foreheads or on their hands. And they lived and reigned with Christ for a thousand years.

REVELATION 20:4

*F*ollowing the defeat of the opposing armies, Christ returns and judges the nations (Matthew 25:31–46) and separates the "sheep" nations from the "goat" nations. The rebels (goats) are purged and are sent into judgment and punishment for their disbelief (Matthew 25:41–46). Then, those who've been converted—the "sheep"—by accepting the message that the 144,000 Jews preached during the Tribulation hour, enter into the millennial, or thousand-year reign of Christ.

Included in the hosts who go into this great millennial hour are the Jews of Old Testament times. They were resurrected at the conclusion of the Tribulation (Daniel 12:2) so they, along with the raised Tribulation saints (Revelation 20:4–6), might be participants in the Millennium on earth.

Prophecy Promises

THE WORLD DURING
THE MILLENNIUM

He shall judge between the nations, and rebuke many people; they shall beat their swords into plowshares, and their spears into pruning hooks; nation shall not lift up sword against nation, neither shall they learn war anymore.

ISAIAH 2:4

Then the eyes of the blind shall be opened, and the ears of the deaf shall be unstopped. Then the lame man shall leap like a deer, and the tongue of the dumb sing. For waters shall burst forth in the wilderness, and streams in the desert. The parched ground shall become a pool, and the thirsty land springs of water; in the habitation of jackals, where each lay, there shall be grass with reeds and rushes.

ISAIAH 35:5–7

God's Promises of Prophecy

$\mathcal{M}$*illennium* is composed of two Latin words: *Mille,* "thousand," and *annum,* meaning "year." Literally, then, *Millennium* means *one thousand years.* It will be a time of utopia—a peace such as the world has never known. The wolf will lie down with the lamb (Isaiah 11:6). War will be a thing of the past. Why? Because the Prince of Peace is with us and *of the increase of His government and peace there will be no end* (Isaiah 9:6, 7).

During this time, the world's motto will be HOLINESS TO THE LORD (Zechariah 14:20, 21). Universal righteousness will flood the world during this glorious hour. Everything will be beautiful, calm, and tranquil—the government a stable, warless *theocracy,* with Messiah, the Lord Jesus Christ, ruling as King (Daniel 7:13, 14).

DIFFERING VIEWS OF
THE MILLENNIUM

For the LORD knows the way of the righteous, but the way of the ungodly shall perish.

PSALM 1:6

For I will gather all nations to battle against Jerusalem; the city shall be taken, the houses rifled, and the women ravished. Half of the city shall go into captivity, and the residue of the people shall not be cut off from the city. . . . And in that day His feet will stand on the Mount of Olives, which faces Jerusalem on the east. And the Mount of Olives shall be split in two, from east to west, making a very large valley; half of the mountain shall move toward the north and half of it toward the south. . . . And it shall come to pass that everyone who is left of all the nations which came against Jerusalem shall go up from year to year to worship the King, the LORD of hosts, and to keep the Feast of Tabernacles.

ZECHARIAH 14:2, 4, 16

He will come and save you. Then the eyes of the blind shall be opened, and the ears of the deaf shall be unstopped.

ISAIAH 35:4, 5

*A*millennialism takes the position that there is *no* millennium. Its advocates deny the message of Isaiah 11:7 and scores of other Old Testament texts. This theological position symbolizes and regards as figurative such passages as Isaiah 35:4, 5. Amillennialists believe that Christ comes, destroys the world—and that's the end of everything. Amillennialists are the present dooms-day prophets proclaiming the world's end.

Post-millennialism postulates that Christ will come after the thousand-year period is completed. Proponents of this view believe the world will become better and better until perfection is finally achieved—after which Christ will appear. This view, apparently, does not regard 2 Timothy 3:13 as valid, *But evil men and imposters will grow worse and worse, deceiving and being deceived.* *Dominion theology* is another name for this position, one currently so untenable that few espouse its teaching.

Pre-millennialism, the position taken in this book, states that the literal, bodily return of Christ will precede the Millennium—the thousand years of peace on earth under the rule of Jesus Christ, the King of kings.

"THAT FINAL DAY"

But, beloved, do not forget this one thing, that with the Lord one day is as a thousand years, and a thousand years as one day.

2 PETER 3:8

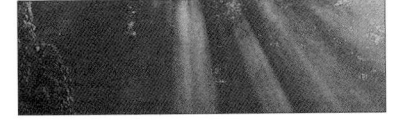

And I saw thrones, and they sat on them, and judgment was committed to them. Then I saw the souls of those who had been beheaded for their witness to Jesus and for the word of God, who had not worshiped the beast or his image, and had not received his mark on their foreheads or on their hands. And they lived and reigned with Christ for a thousand years.

REVELATION 20:4

The Millennium itself is *that final day of 1,000 years! One day with the Lord is as a thousand years, and a thousand years as one day* (2 Peter 3:8). Revelation 20:4 declares that *they [the returning, resurrected, and raised saints] lived and reigned with Christ for a thousand years.* Our present calendar indicates this prophecy is soon to be fulfilled.

From Adam to the birth of Jesus Christ, approximately 4,000 years have transpired—or figuratively "four days." Then, from the birth of Christ almost "two more days" have passed. According to God's Word, we are approaching the culmination of the final two "days" for a total of 6,000 years, or the six "days" proposed by Peter. We are rapidly approaching the completion of that six-day period and may soon enter the millennial age.

Calendar changes make it impossible to know the day or hour (Matthew 24:36).

CHARACTERISTICS OF THE MILLENNIUM

For unto us a Child is born, unto us a Son is given; and the government will be upon His shoulder. And His name will be called Wonderful, Counselor, Mighty God, Everlasting Father, Prince of Peace.

ISAIAH 9:6

You have multiplied the nation and increased its joy; they rejoice before You according to the joy in harvest, and as men rejoice when they divide the spoil.

ISAIAH 9:3

I will restore your judges as at the first, and your counselors as at the beginning. Afterward you shall be called the city of righteousness, the faithful city.

ISAIAH 1:26

For the earth will be filled with the knowledge of the glory of the LORD, as the waters cover the sea.

HABAKKUK 2:14

And the inhabitant will not say, "I am sick"; the people who dwell in it will be forgiven their iniquity.

ISAIAH 33:24

*F*ive specific ingredients will characterize the Millennium:

1. *Peace*—because Christ *the Prince of Peace reigns* (Isaiah 2:4; 9:6).
2. *Joy*—because there will be no war. There will be no selfishness. People will share what they have with others (Isaiah 9:3).
3. *Holiness*—because the rule of law will return—as it was in the beginning. Doors will remain unlocked. People will feel safe. All will be well with the world (Isaiah 1:26, 27; Jeremiah 32:23).
4. *Knowledge*—because the focus will be on the glory of the Lord, not man's achievements. The message of the goodness of God that Christians had been trying to convey for centuries will now be the subject of the evening news (Isaiah 11:1, 2, 9; Habakkuk 2:14).
5. *Health*—because no one will be sick. People will be forgiven for their sins, as they see in great detail the close tie between their former estrangement from God and their previous poor physical health (Isaiah 33:24; 35:5; Revelation 22:2).

WORLD HEADQUARTERS DURING THE MILLENNIUM

And in that day His feet will stand on the Mount of Olives, which faces Jerusalem on the east. And the Mount of Olives shall be split in two from east to west, making a very large valley; half of the mountain shall move toward the north and half of it toward the south.

ZECHARIAH 14:4

Many people shall come and say, "Come, and let us go up to the mountain of the LORD, to the house of the God of Jacob; He will teach us His ways, and we shall walk in His paths." For out of Zion shall go forth the law, and the word of the LORD from Jerusalem.

ISAIAH 2:3

He will be great, and will be called the Son of the Highest; and the Lord God will give Him the throne of His father David. And He will reign over the house of Jacob forever, and of His kingdom there will be no end.

LUKE 1:32, 33

*D*uring the Millennium the world headquarters will be located in Jerusalem—the sight where the Lord touches down at His second coming to earth and the city from which He will rule. When Christ comes on that great day, the gates of Jerusalem will open wide to welcome the coming King (see Psalm 24). Psalm 24 also describes His reign; Psalm 96 indicates that His coming will be to judge the earth.

The Scripture predicts that at the coming of Christ His enemies will be made His footstool, and that during the Millennium, multitudes will come from the uttermost parts of the earth to visit the holy city (Zechariah 14:16).

WHAT WILL CHRISTIANS DO DURING THE MILLENNIUM?

I saw a new heaven and a new earth, for the first heaven and the first earth had passed away. Also there was no more sea. Then I, John, saw the holy city, New Jerusalem, coming down out of heaven from God, prepared as a bride adorned for her husband.

REVELATION 21:1, 2

And everyone who has this hope in Him purifies himself, just as He is pure.

1 JOHN 3:3

For now we see in a mirror, dimly, but then face to face. Now I know in part, but then I shall know just as I also am known.

1 CORINTHIANS 13:12

God's Promises of Prophecy

Before space travel, many scoffed at the scientific possibility of space stations and inner-galactic communities "hovering" over the earth, "flying machines" where people would be able to live and work for extended periods of time. No one is laughing any longer, and the Bible clearly teaches that Christians will actually *hover* over the Holy Land in the New Jerusalem (Revelation 21: 22). Further, we will be able to travel as quickly as thought itself. We will think something—and we'll be there *instantly*. We will traverse back and forth from the Holy City to earth as easily as we now walk from one room in our home to another.

When Jesus was on earth, we know that He could go through a closed door if He chose to do so. In like manner, we will be able to do the same because *we shall be like Him* (1 John 3:2). We will be able to do what He does. We will have the knowledge that He has. We shall know as we are known. For Christians it will the greatest day in history (1 Corinthians 13:12).

WHAT HAPPENS AFTER THE MILLENNIUM?

But the day of the Lord will come as a thief in the night, in which the heavens will pass away with a great noise, and the elements will melt with fervent heat; both the earth and the works that are in it shall be burned up.

2 PETER 3:10

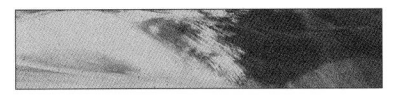

And I saw an angel coming down from heaven, having the key of the bottomless pit and a great chain in his hand. He laid hold of the dragon, that serpent of old, who is the Devil and Satan, and bound him for a thousand years.

REVELATION 20:1, 2

After the Millennium we find the world purified through fire (2 Peter 3:10), after which time there will emerge a regenerated or renewed *heaven and earth* (Revelation 21:1). In studying Revelation 20:7–9, however, we see that after the Millennium Satan is released from the pit and manages to lead a rebellion against Christ. The question then arises: *How can such an event take place after 1,000 years of Christ's reign on earth?* We must remember that during the Millennium the children born still have old natures and hardened hearts. That is why Christ has to rule the nations with a *rod of iron* to maintain control of the world's population. Yes, He breaks them (their stubborn wills) with a rod of iron (Psalm 2:9).

The earth's inhabitants still can—and do—produce children during the Millennium, but because Satan is bound (Revelation 20:1, 2), there is no Satanic power to influence these mortals, their children, grandchildren and great-grandchildren. However, the children born *during the Millennium,* as already mentioned, still possess the old Adamic, or sin-prone, nature. Only because Christ rules with a rod of iron are they kept under control during that thousand-year period. When Satan is again unleashed on earth, these are the very ones who are deceived into joining Satan's rebellion.

Prophecy Promises
THE FINAL
REBELLION

Now when the thousand years have expired, Satan will be released from his prison.

REVELATION 20:7

They went up on the breadth of the earth and surrounded the camp of the saints and the beloved city. And fire came down from God out of heaven and devoured them. The devil, who deceived them, was cast into the lake of fire and brimstone where the beast and the false prophet are. And they will be tormented day and night forever and ever.

REVELATION 20:9, 10

After 1,000 years of being bound, Satan is loosed for a brief period of time to test earth's inhabitants (see Revelation 20:7). God has always wanted every human being to follow Him by his or her own free will. Thus, these "millennial children" will be severely tested after being with Jesus and His great outpouring of love and compassion for 1,000 years. Then millions still make the decision to follow Satan. The human heart is so wicked that after 1,000 years of living with the tender loving Savior, mankind rebels.

This is much the same response that Jesus received when He first came to earth. Some accepted Him, but the multitudes did not: *they preferred to go the way of Satan.* Now, during this final rebellion, an insurrection organized and led by Satan, causes all hell to break loose on earth. Soon, however, fire comes down from God and devours Satan and his followers. Following this, God's Word states that *The devil, who deceived them, was cast into the lake of fire and brimstone where the beast and the false prophet are. And they will be tormented day and night forever and ever* (Revelation 20:9).

THE JUDGMENT SEAT OF CHRIST

For no other foundation can anyone lay than that which is laid, which is Jesus Christ. Now if anyone builds on this foundation with gold, silver, precious stones, wood, hay, straw, each one's work will become clear; for the Day will declare it, because it will be revealed by fire; and the fire will test each one's work of what sort it is. If anyone's work which he has built on it endures, he will receive a reward. If anyone's work is burned, he will suffer loss; but he himself will be saved, yet so as through fire.

1 CORINTHIANS 3:11–15

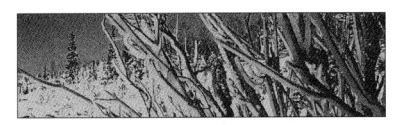

Therefore judge nothing before the time, until the Lord comes, who will both bring to light the hidden things of darkness and reveal the counsels of the hearts. Then each one's praise will come from God.

1 CORINTHIANS 4:5

The Judgment Seat of Christ is one of the most important prophetic teachings in God's Word and is clearly portrayed in 1 Corinthians 3:11–15. It is certain that one cannot lose his or her salvation, only the rewards (note verse 15). Here is a text that incorporates the terms "lost" and "saved" in one breath. If the believer's work of service upon earth has been of impure motivation and self-love, the fire of God reduces these works to perishable wood, hay, and stubble. As a result, all of such a person's life service is lost. However, even though believers suffer great loss, they themselves remain saved—by fire or *by the skin of their teeth.*

However, service and "works" done with the pure motive of glorifying Jesus Christ will be rewarded with gold, silver, and precious stones. There will be crowns to be laid at the feet of Jesus (Revelation 4:10, 11). God takes these two kinds of works and puts them in the fires of testing. The reality of this future judgment event should make every Christian keenly aware of his or her motivation for service in the here and now.

BELIEVERS APPEAR BEFORE CHRIST IN CONFIDENCE

But why do you judge your brother? Or why do you show contempt for your brother? For we shall all stand before the judgment seat of Christ. For it is written: "As I live, says the LORD, every knee shall bow to Me, and every tongue shall confess to God."

ROMANS 14:10, 11

And now, little children, abide in Him, that when He appears, we may have confidence and not be ashamed before Him at His coming.

1 JOHN 2:28

And whatever you do in word or deed, do all in the name of the Lord Jesus, giving thanks to God the Father through Him.

COLOSSIANS 3:17

$\mathcal{G}$od will investigate the motives behind the works of every Christian who appears before Him. As we've already noted, if there is even one iota of self-glorification behind any act of service, the rewards for that Christian will be sparse indeed—if any (see Matthew 6:1–6, 16–19). The confident ones who appear before the Judgment Seat will see their works of gold, silver, and precious stones untouched by the fire of testing. Genuine service for the Savior will result in heaven's "Oscars" and "Emmys" being presented to those who build upon (1) the foundation of Christ (see 1 Corinthians 3:11), and (2) the glory of Christ: *And whatever you do in word or deed, do all in the name of the Lord Jesus, giving thanks to God the Father through Him* (Colossians 3:17).

Prophecy Promises

THOSE WHO ARE TURNED AWAY FROM THE HOLY CITY

But the cowardly, unbelieving, abominable, murderers, sexually immoral, sorcerers, idolaters, and all liars shall have their part in the lake which burns with fire and brimstone, which is the second death.

REVELATION 21:8

But outside are dogs and sorcerers and sexually immoral and murderers and idolaters, and whoever loves and practices a lie. "I, Jesus, have sent My angel to testify to you these things in the churches. I am the Root and the Offspring of David, and the Bright and Morning Star."

REVELATION 22:15, 16

Do you not know that the unrighteous will not inherit the kingdom of God? Do not be deceived. Neither fornicators, nor idolaters, nor adulterers, nor homosexuals, nor sodomites, nor thieves, nor covetous, nor drunkards, nor revilers, nor extortioners will inherit the kingdom of God.

1 CORINTHIANS 6:9, 10

God's Promises of Prophecy

There are a minimum of thirty-nine "types" of individuals who will be turned away from heaven at the final judgment. Here are ten:

1. *The fearful*—those who do not accept Christ to escape being ridiculed (Matthew 10:32).

2. *Unbelievers*—those who do not believe and receive the Lord Jesus Christ (John 8:24).

3. *The abominable*—those who engage in wicked practices (Titus 1:16).

4. *Sexually immoral*—those who engage in fornication or consort with prostitutes (Ephesians 5:5–8).

5. *Sorcerers*—The word *sorcery* comes from the Greek word *pharmakeia* and means "an enchantment with drugs."

6. *Idolaters*—those who worship or reverence anyone or anything other than the true and living God.

7. *Liars*—(John 8:44).

8. *Dogs*—false teachers (2 Peter 2:22).

9. *The Unrighteous*—those who live a life of sin without repentance (1 John 1:9; 3:8).

10. *Deceivers*—those who purposely mislead or betray others (2 Timothy 3:13).

GOD'S JUDGMENT

O LORD, You have searched me and known me. You know my sitting down and my rising up, You understand my thought afar off. You comprehend my path and my lying down, and are acquainted with all my ways. For there is not a word on my tongue, but behold, O LORD, You know it altogether.

PSALM 139:1–4

Then the Spirit of the LORD fell upon me, and said to me, "Speak! 'Thus says the LORD: "Thus you have said, O house of Israel; for I know the things that come into your mind."'"

EZEKIEL 11:5

And I saw the dead, small and great, standing before God, and books were opened. And another book was opened, which is the Book of Life. And the dead were judged according to their works, by the things which were written in the books.

REVELATION 20:12

*A*ccording to the words of
Scripture, throughout our lifetime God
has amassed a detailed record of our
earthly activities. God knows all things
about us (Psalm 139), and not a single
detail of our lives—not even our
"thought life"—has escaped Him
(Ezekiel 11:5). God is omniscient. He
knows everything about everything and
knows all things about all things. The
Scripture also informs us that God
keeps good books (Revelation 20:12)!

The good news is that the ungodly
(Romans 5:6) can be totally cleansed
and forgiven. Since Christ *died for our
sins* (1 Corinthians 15:3) and His
precious blood *cleanses from all sin*
(1 John 1:7), our sins are then forgiven
and forgotten forever (Hebrews 8:12;
10:17). Because of these glorious
truths, *There is therefore now no
condemnation to those who are in Christ
Jesus* (Romans 8:1).

AFTER THE DESTRUCTION OF THE OLD EARTH AND HEAVENS

For behold, I create new heavens and a new earth; and the former shall not be remembered or come to mind.

ISAIAH 65:17

Now I saw a new heaven and a new earth, for the first heaven and the first earth had passed away. Also there was no more sea. Then I, John, saw the holy city, New Jerusalem, coming down out of heaven from God, prepared as a bride adorned for her husband.

REVELATION 21:1, 2

Nevertheless we, according to His promise, look for new heavens and a new earth in which righteousness dwells.

2 PETER 3:13

And he carried me away in the Spirit to a great and high mountain, and showed me the great city, the holy Jerusalem, descending out of heaven from God.

REVELATION 21:10

*F*ollowing the purification of the old earth and heavens, God restores and renovates heaven and earth. This will occur after this present heaven and earth are dissolved at the close of the Millennium—Christ's thousand-year reign on earth. Since Israel's covenants guarantee God's chosen people a nation forever, *and a king and spiritual blessing unending,* there must therefore be a place for the inhabitants of Israel to dwell. The renovation and restoration of earth plus heavens one and two make our earth the scenario for the eternal kingdom of God on earth (Revelation 22:1–8).

The ultimate destiny of the Church saints is related more to a Person (Christ) than to a place. The place is important (Jerusalem) but is now overshadowed by the Person into whose presence the believer is taken (John 14:3; Colossians 3:4). Remember heaven is located wherever Christ rules (Luke 1:33).

Prophecy Promises
WE DO NOT REALLY HAVE TO DIE

For God so loved the world that He gave His only begotten Son, that whoever believes in Him should not perish but have everlasting life.

JOHN 3:16

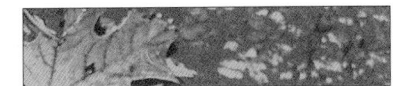

Paul, a bondservant of God and an apostle of Jesus Christ, according to the faith of God's elect and the acknowledging of the truth which accords godliness, in hope [the Greek word guarantee] of eternal life which God, who cannot lie, promised before time began.

TITUS 1:1, 2

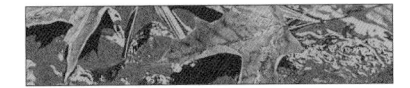

We are confident, yes, well pleased rather to be absent from the body and to be present with the Lord.

2 CORINTHIANS 5:8

*W*hen we put our faith in Christ as Savior, at that moment we receive the ultimate in God's grace—the marvelous gift of eternal life. John 3:15 reminds us that *whoever believes in Him should not perish but have eternal life.* Pure and simple, it means that once we have been born again through the blood of Jesus Christ *we will not die.* In the end, *to be absent from the body is to be present with the Lord,* instantaneously and simultaneously.

This is why Paul says in Philippians 1:21 that *to die is gain.* We close our eyes here—and open them instantaneously over there. That is eternal life. Perhaps as you've read the seventy prophecies in this book (and there are thousands more) you've wondered about the state of your own soul before God. It may be that you're not sure you are ready for that final day when Jesus returns to take His own to be with Him forever. On the other hand, you may have read these prophecies with a glad heart, knowing beyond a doubt in whom you have believed—confident that you are ready for that final day.

Maranatha

D0443285